Contents

Introduction

The word 'Pompom' is derived from the French word *pompon*. The French and Belgians have been using pompoms to adorn naval uniforms for centuries; Italians to decorate wedding shoes and Roman Catholic clergy to ornament the biretta – a square-shaped hat. The coloured pompom in the centre signifies the wearer's rank within the priesthood.

More recent years have seen the pompom become a fashion statement, adorning many a golf or beanie hat, keeping small children occupied for hours winding yarn over two cardboard rings, or simply cascading from beautifully trimmed curtains. The humble pompom has now reinvented itself! Pompoms are not just to decorate hats or soft furnishings – they can be sculpted into wonderful shapes and transformed into something quite spectacular.

In this book I will show you how to make a rabbit called Ruby, a bear called Ben and a fabulous array of pompom creations from pumpkins and pillows to gift toppers and jewellery. All of the designs are easy to follow and come with step-by-step instructions, using the traditional cardboard ring method or the more modern plastic pompom maker which clips together. Pompom making is portable too, so, makers and yarn at the ready, and get creating – please pompom responsibly!

Techniques

Making pompoms the traditional way

1 Cut out two identical cardboard discs to the diameter of the intended pompom. Mark out a smaller circle in the centre of each disc. This will form a hole to allow yarn to be passed through. As a rule of thumb, this circle should be half the diameter of the outer circle. Cut the inner circles out.

2 Hold the two cardboard discs together and start to wind your chosen yarn around the rings. Cover the ring entirely until the hole in the centre has almost disappeared.

3 With fabric scissors, cut though the yarn between the cardboard discs around the outer edge. Cut around the entire circumference, releasing all of the yarn and revealing the cardboard discs.

4 Tie a spare piece of yarn between the discs to secure the middle of the pompom.

5 Once knotted securely, tear the cardboard to release the pompom.

6 Finish by trimming the pompom into a neat ball.

Making pompoms with a plastic maker

1 Wrap the yarn around one half of the pompom maker.

2 Continue wrapping until you have created a thick layer, then start wrapping yarn around the other half.

3 When finished, close the pompom maker and cut through all the yarns.

4 Wrap a length of yarn two or three times round the middle of the pompom maker. Pull tight and knot securely.

5 Release the pompom from the pompom maker and trim into a neat ball.

Tools and templates
For all projects in this book you will need fabric scissors and thread snips. Other tools required are listed on the project pages.

Some of the projects require templates. All templates in this book are reproduced at half their actual size. You will therefore need to enlarge them to 200 per cent using a photocopier.

Sizing
A4 is used as a size reference in the Flag Cushions, the Christmas Tea Light, the Daisy Decorations and the Cup and Ball Toy. A4 is equivalent to 210 x 297mm (8¼ x 11¾in)

Flag Cushions

Materials:

1 x 100g ball each of red and white yarn

Red and blue cotton fabric: 3 x A4 pieces for each cushion; one extra A4 piece of blue for Stars and Stripes cushion

Star-shaped metal studs, 10mm (³/₈in)

White felt strips, about 5 x 60cm (2 x 23½in)

White, red and blue matching sewing threads

Toy stuffing

Tools:

A4 paper

Paper scissors

Tailor's chalk

Size 25mm (1in) pompom maker

Sewing machine

Iron

Ruler

Pins

Sewing needle

Note:
see page 7 for exact A4 dimensions.

Instructions:

1 For both cushions, use an A4 sheet of paper as a template for the bases. Lay the A4 template on to the cotton, mark out three pieces using tailor's chalk, and cut them out. Place two pieces of fabric, with right sides facing down, in a landscape position. Fold the left-hand side of the rectangle approximately 10cm (4in) towards the middle of the fabric and press flat along the crease. Repeat this step with the second piece. These form the entry flaps on the cushion back.

2 For the Union Jack, place the remaining A4 cotton piece righth side up in a landscape position. Fold it from left to right matching the edges perfectly. Where the fabric folds in the middle, mark with chalk. Repeat this process but this time folding it from top to bottom. Join the marks with chalk. This will give you central guidelines on which to place the felt strips. Pin the felt from left to right along the chalk guidelines and sew into place using a sewing machine. Repeat along the top to bottom guideline. Sew along both felt strips as close to the felt edge as you can.

3 Using a 25mm (1in) pompom maker and red yarn, make up seven pompoms to run from top to bottom and ten from left to right (five each side of the vertical line of pompoms). Trim the pompoms into neat rounds and place them down and across the centre of the ribbon. Position them carefully, hand sew them into place (sew directly through the pompoms to ensure a secure attachment).

4 To make the four diagonal white and red lines of pompoms, wind two rows of red yarn on one half of the maker, then add white yarn on top of the red to complete. The second half should be wound solely in white. Make six pompoms for each of the four diagonal lines. Trim, and sew into position. Align the red yarn in each pompom to create a stripe of red as shown in the photograph.

5 For the Stars and Stripes cushion, take two of the A4 pieces of red fabric and follow Step 2 to form the entry flaps for the cushion. Lay the remaining red A4 sheet right side up in a landscape position. With a ruler and chalk, mark the first line 3.5cm (1³/₈in) from the top and thereafter at 4.5cm (1¾in) intervals (you should have four lines).

6 Cut out a rectangle in blue cotton measuring 15 x 9cm (6 x 3½in). With the right side facing down and in a landscape position, press towards the centre 1cm (½in) along both top and left edges. Place in the top left-hand corner, right side up on to the red cotton, matching raw edges. Sew along the pressed sides with a sewing machine to attach it to the cushion. Add the metal star studs in rows and equally spaced from left to right. Make up approximately twenty-eight pompoms in white yarn. Trim into neat balls and sew into position along the chalk guidelines.

7 To finish both cushions, start by lining up one of the back pieces to the cushion front with right sides facing. Match up the corners and raw edges, then pin and sew to secure. Repeat this process in the same manner for the opposite side. Snip the corners and pull the cushion through. Tease out the corners and stuff to the desired plumpness.

Crazy Cupcakes

Materials:

1 x 100g ball each of light brown and red yarn

Scrap of yarn in a bright colour

Small amounts of white and yellow felt

Tools:

Paper and pinking shears

Tailor's chalk

Size 25mm (1in) and 45mm (1¾in) pompom makers

Pins

Sewing needle

Glue gun

Card for templates

Instructions:

1 Enlarge the templates provided below by 200 per cent and transfer them to a piece of card. Cut out and set aside.

2 With red yarn, make up one 25mm (1in) pompom. This will form a cherry for the top of the cupcake. Using light brown yarn and a 45mm (1¾in) pompom maker, make a larger pompom. Trim and shape each one into a neat ball and set aside.

3 Lay the cupcake case template on to some yellow felt and mark out with chalk. With fabric scissors cut out the sides and base curve of the case. To create the serrated top of the case, carefully cut this top curve with pinking shears (shown by the zigzag red line on the template). Bring the short edges together, overlapping by

about 4mm (¹/₈in), and pin to hold. Hand sew with a running stitch to secure in place, and remove the pin.

4 Take a scrap of bright-coloured yarn and wrap it around the felt ring. Use the jagged tops as a guide. Leave two jagged points in between each line of yarn. Continue to wrap the yarn around the whole case until you reach the start. Tie both loose ends of yarn inside the case to secure. Trim the ends and rearrange evenly around the base of the case.

5 Cut out the icing shape using white felt. Sew the cherry to the middle to secure. Assemble the cupcake by glueing the brown pompom into the case, followed by the icing topper complete with cherry.

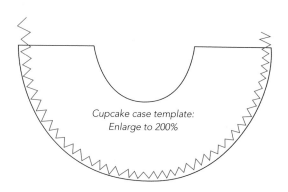

Cupcake case template:
Enlarge to 200%

Icing template:
Enlarge to 200%

Valentine Heart

Materials:

1 x 100g ball of red yarn

1 x wire dry cleaner's
coat hanger

Red satin ribbon 3mm ($^1/_8$in)
wide x 1m (39½in) long

Tools:

Size 25mm (1in) pompom maker

Wire cutters

Pliers

Permanent pen

Instructions:

1 Make up 33 pompoms using red yarn and a 25mm (1in) pompom maker. You may need more, depending on the size of your coat hanger when you have made it into the heart frame. Trim each pompom into a neat ball using fabric scissors and set aside.

2 To make the heart frame, first remove the hook top of the hanger with the wire cutters. Take care while doing this, keeping fingers well away when cutting. You will be left with a three-sided wire frame. Mark the middle of the long side with a pen. This is the first bending point. Using the pliers, bend the wire at the marked point, bringing the two shorter sides down. The hanger will be in the shape of a letter 'w'. The next stage is to begin to form the heart shape by straightening the hanger's existing curves with pliers. The hanger will now form the shape of an upside down 'v'.

3 Turn the 'v' so that it is the right way up, and mark 10cm along each side of the wire from the point of the 'v'. From these marks, begin bending the wire with the pliers to form the two lobes of the heart. When you are happy with the shape, bend a small loop at the tip of one of the cut ends.

4 Thread all of the pompoms on to the wire. You may have to tease them on. Make sure you go straight through the middles. Once they are all mounted, make a second small loop on the remaining cut end. Interlock this loop with the other one to secure the heart frame together. Push the pompoms towards the join to hide it.

5 Omitting the central pompom that covers the join, count four pompoms from the middle. Tie the red ribbon in between the fourth and fifth pompom on either side, then tie the ribbon ends together in a bow to form a hanger.

His 'n' Hers Gift Toppers

Materials:

Green (two shades) and pink yarn scraps

Black grosgrain ribbon 1.5cm wide x 1m long
(½ x 39½in)

White sewing thread

Gift wrap with desired ribbons

Cream dress net

2 x small toy cars

Styrofoam balls, 1 x 2.5cm (1in) and
1 x 4cm (1½in)

Scraps of thin pink ribbon

Tools:

Size 25mm (1in), 35mm (1³/₈in), 45mm
(1¾in), 65mm (2½in) and 85mm (3³/₈in)
pompom makers

Hand sewing needles

Glue gun

Instructions:

1 For the green gift topper, start by making
the following sizes of pompoms: 1 x 85mm
(3³/₈in), 1 x 65mm (2½in), 1 x 45mm (1¾in) and
2 x 35mm (1³/₈in). Make these in two different
shades of green. Trim into neat balls. Wrap the
black ribbon around three of the pompoms
(the two largest and one of the smallest)
to measure and cut an amount off for each
pompom to form the road. Add the white road
markings with a simple, large running stitch to
the centre of each ribbon. Attach the ribbon to
the base of each pompom using a glue gun.

2 Wrap the gift with your desired paper and
add ribbon if required. Arrange the hills and
cars into position and secure them using the
glue gun.

3 For the pink gift topper, use pink yarn to
make the following sizes of pompoms: 1
x 85mm (3³/₈in) and 2 x 45mm (1¾in). Trim
to neaten and place to one side (for these
pompoms do not cut off the tied yarn as this
will be used to secure them to the parcel). Cut
out two squares of dress net on the double
measuring 25 x 25cm (9¾ x 9¾in) and 15 x
15cm (6 x 6in). Wrap the dress net around the

styrofoam balls and tie with the pink ribbon to
encase each ball securely, leaving enough slack
to form ties.

4 Wrap the gift with your desired paper and
ribbon. Arrange the pompoms and encased
balls into a design on top and tie into position
using the ribbon tied around the parcel to
anchor it. To finish, trim the excess ties to
desired lengths.

Dainty Dove

Materials:

White yarn

Brown yarn scraps

Brown chenille stick

White pre-wired feathers

Red felt

White thread

Blue mounted sew-on
gemstones

Tools:

Paper scissors

Size 35mm ($1^3/_8$in) and 65mm
(2½in) pompom makers

Sewing needles

Pointed tip pliers

Tailor's chalk

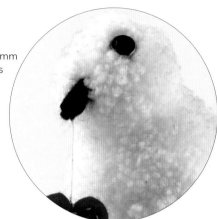

Instructions:

1 Enlarge the heart template below by 200 per cent and pin it to the doubled red felt. Cut out the two heart shapes, sew them together with a decorative running stitch, and set them to one side.

2 In the meantime, make one 35mm ($1^3/_8$in) pompom for the dove's head and one 65mm (2½in) pompom for the body in white yarn. Trim the smaller pompom into a neat ball and set aside. Instead of a ball, you will need to trim the larger pompom into an egg shape. Take your time doing this for better results – a little at a time. With the body completed, attach the head securely to one of the pointed ends with yarn.

3 Add some of the white feathers to form a tail. Push the wire through the body until it re-appears out of the other side. Trim the wire end and use the pointed pliers to bend it round and twist into the body, burying the wire out of sight. Finish the tail and use the same method when forming the wings. Keep adding feathers until you are happy with the look.

4 To form a beak, cut off a 3cm (1¼in) length of pipe cleaner and wrap the brown yarn around it. Bend it in half, bringing both ends together and wrap more yarn around the whole thing (do not make this too bulky). Secure the yarn and sew the beak into position.

5 Attach the sew-on gemstones as the dove's eyes to the head with a needle and thread. Then attach the heart to the beak with some white thread, making sure there is enough slack to allow it to hang.

Note: This item is not a toy – do not allow children to play with it.

*Heart template:
Enlarge to 200%*

Jolly Bunting

Materials:

Assorted colours of yarn

Blue bias binding 25mm (1in) wide and the length of your choice

Grosgrain ribbon 1cm (½in) wide; allow 18cm (7in) per pompom, in assorted colours

Tools:

Size 25mm (1in) pompom maker

Sewing machine

Iron

Ruler

Pins

Instructions:

1 With a 25mm (1in) pompom maker, make up as many pompoms as you require. Use as many different-coloured yarns as you can. Trim and shape into neat balls and put to one side.

2 Press the length of bias binding in half lengthways, taking care to match the edges. Now insert one end of grosgrain ribbon, pre-cut to 18cm (7in), and pin. Make sure you leave enough slack bias binding to form ties at the start and finish of your bunting. With one end of the ribbon secured, insert the second end 5cm (2in) away from the first. Repeat this step until all of the ribbons are in place. Each ribbon 'v' should be spaced at regular intervals measuring 5cm (2in).

3 Set a sewing machine to a medium stitch and sew along the open edge of the bias binding, trapping the ribbon ends within. Try and sew as close to the edge as possible.

4 Add a contrasting pompom to each ribbon tip and hang.

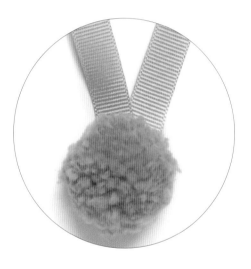

Princess Tiara and Wand

Materials:

1 x 100g ball each of white, pink and lilac yarn

Plastic hairband

1 x dry cleaner's metal coat hanger

Yellow satin ribbon 3mm (1/8in) wide and approx. 5m (5½yd) long

Slim garden cane

Florist's wire

White sewing thread

Tools:

Tailor's chalk

Size 25mm (1in) and 65mm (2½in) pompom makers

Ruler

Wire cutters

Pointed tip pliers

Pliers

Permanent marker

Knitting dolly (hand-cranked)

Awl

Sewing needle

Instructions:

1 Cut off the hooked part of the coat hanger, keeping your fingers well away whilst doing so. Mark the middle point of the longest side of the wire with a pen. Use this mark to bend the first point in the tiara with pliers (so the pen mark will form the top of the middle peak). Straighten out the wire on either side of the original hanger shape and create the two other peaks to sit either side of the taller middle peak. All of the points along the base, including the cut ends, should run in a straight line. Gently shape this line into a horseshoe shape, to follow the curve of the hairband.

2 Using a knitting dolly, make up around 6–7 metres (6½–7½yd) of braid using pink yarn. Thread the tiara wire through the centre of the braid until completely hidden. Cut off the excess braid to use later. Now form two small loops on the cut ends of the wire with pliers to secure the wire frame to the hairband. Make two small holes in the hairband on either side with an awl, 5cm (2in) away from the tips, and equidistant from the sides. Secure the wire frame to the hairband using strong florist's wire. Snip off excess wire and flatten off.

3 Divide the remaining braid in two. Stretch open one end and pull it over the hairband tip to anchor it. Wrap the braid around the band to hide the plastic to halfway along the hairband. Repeat this step on the other side. Hide the braid ends at the back of the hairband once

they meet, cutting off the excess, and secure with needle and thread. Make up nine 25mm (1in) pompoms in white and three in lilac yarn. Use to decorate and finish the tiara.

4 Using both pink and lilac yarn, make one 65mm (2½in) pompom. Once you have cut through the yarn, secure the centre of the pompom in the usual manner, but do not remove the maker at this point. Take a small length of yellow ribbon and tie on smaller lengths (the knot should be in the centre of the smaller lengths). When this yellow ribbon looks fluffy enough, tie into the maker and pompom centre. Remove the maker and trim the pompom, taking care not to cut the ribbon.

5 Cover a small length of cane with the remaining braid and secure one end into the wand head made in step 4 with a needle and yarn. To finish, make a pink 25mm (1in) pompom and attach to the opposite end.

Hanging Lantern

Materials:

1 x 100g ball of red yarn

Two pieces of red felt 6 x 6cm (2¼ x 2¼in)

Yellow embroidery thread

Florist's wire

2 x styrofoam rings 9cm (3½in) in diameter

Red satin ribbon 3mm x 1m (¹/₈ x 39½in)

Battery-operated tea light (optional)

Tools:

Tailor's chalk

Size 25mm (1in) pompom maker

Pointed tipped pliers

Ruler

Knitting doll (hand-cranked)

Compasses

Glue gun

Instructions:

1 Make up 25 pompoms in red yarn with a 25mm (1in) pompom maker. Trim into neat balls and set aside. You will need five pompoms per arm of the lantern.

2 Use the rest of the red yarn to knit up 4 metres (4¼yd) of braid using a knitting dolly. If you use a hand-cranked version, this will knit up very quickly. Divide the braid in half. Use the braid to wrap round the styrofoam rings, hiding the white bits. When you have completely covered the ring, snip off the excess and secure with a glue gun. Tuck the loose ends under the wound braid to hide them. As an option, you could paint the styrofoam rings red first, so that you would not have to wrap the braid round so tightly to hide the white.

3 Hold one ring and insert a length of florist's wire from the bottom of the ring and out through the top. Pull the wire through, leaving a small section. Roll this section into a loop with a set of pointed pliers, flatten on to the ring base and hide it under the braid. Continue until you have five wires, equally spaced, to create arms.

4 Keep the wires straight and thread five pompoms on to each wire. Place the remaining ring on to the top of the wire tips and thread the ring on to all five. Push the ring down towards the pompoms. Snip the excess wire off just above the ring's surface and secure the ends as before (see step 3).

5 Set the compasses to 2.25cm (⁷/₈in), mark a circle on some paper and cut out two circles in red felt. Glue the circles together and set aside.

6 Wrap a small amount of red yarn around four fingers and release the yarn by cutting underneath your little finger. Tie and secure the yarn in the middle. From this middle point, bring the loose ends together and tie the yarn near the top with yellow embroidery thread to create a tassel. Sew the tassel to the centre of the felt circle. Attach the felt circle into the middle of the base ring using a glue gun.

7 Now bend the arms into equal curved shapes and attach the red ribbon to the top to allow you to hang the lantern. Place a battery-operated tea light into the cradle if you wish.

Ruby Rabbit

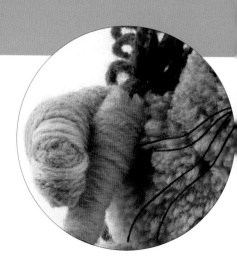

Materials:

1 x 100g ball each of dusky cream and light beige yarn

Orange and green yarn scraps

5 x 30cm (11¾in) chenille sticks

2 x black mounted sew-on gemstones

Pink felt scrap

Black sewing thread

Fabric glue

Tools:

Size 65mm (2½in) and 45mm (1¾in) pompom makers

Small pliers

Sewing needle

Instructions:

1 Ruby's head and body are both made in the same way. Open half of the pompom maker and wind on dusky cream yarn. Fill about three-quarters with this colour. Fill the remaining space with the darker beige yarn. Then fill the empty side using only the beige yarn. Repeat this process until you have completed both sizes. Remove the makers and shape the pompoms into neat balls. Attach the head to the body, sewing through both pompoms with yarn (see photograph for positioning).

2 The legs, arms, ears and carrot are made using the following method. The legs and ears require one full pipe cleaner each, and the arms half a pipe cleaner each. Start by making the legs, using beige yarn. Find the centre of the pipe cleaner and wrap the yarn around. Aim to create a little mound of yarn in the centre. With

the mound complete, bring the pipe cleaner ends together and continue to wrap the yarn. Build the yarn up until you have the desired shape. Secure the yarn by sewing down at the narrower end. The ears should be a slender version of the feet. Complete the arms and ears in the same way. For the carrot, sew dark green yarn into the bulbous tip and leave it loose to resemble the stalks and leaves.

3 Sew together the narrow ends of the legs and ears. You can reduce the length of the parts by bending over these smaller ends if required. Wrap some extra yarn around to hide the join and secure with another stitch. Position the ears and legs to the rear of the body. Once a pleasing shape has been achieved, sew the pieces directly on to the body. Use the same method for the arms; however, before attaching, add some paw detail to the bulbous ends with a little cream yarn.

4 Cut out a small 'twitchy' nose shape from pink felt and add some whiskers with the black sewing thread, which should be secured at the back of the felt nose. Then glue the nose on to the face. Sew on the eyes carefully and, finally, tuck the carrot under Ruby's arm and secure in position with a couple of stitches.

Easter Chicks

Materials:

1 x 100g ball of yellow yarn

Orange yarn scraps

Yellow marabou feathers

Small black beads, approx. 3mm (1/8in) wide

Chenille sticks: 1 x 15cm (6in) per small chick, 1 x 20cm (8in) per large chick, plus 1 x 3cm (1¼in) length per beak

Fabric glue

Tools:

Sizes 25mm (1in), 35mm (1³/8in) and 45mm (1¾in) pompom makers

Ruler

Small wire cutters

Long darning needle

Instructions:

1 For each bird make up the required size of pompoms using yellow yarn. Use one 25mm (1in) and one 35mm (1³/8in) pompom for a small chick, and one 35mm (1³/8in) and one 45mm (1¾in) pompom for a larger chick. Trim the pompoms into neat balls and sew together using matching yarn and a long darning needle. As you sew, flatten the head into the body a little to merge the pompoms.

2 Wrap and cover a 15cm (6in) long pipe cleaner with orange yarn (longer if making the larger bird). When you reach the opposite end, bend the wire to form a foot shape. Sew the tip of the foot to the rear to secure and complete the shape. Repeat this process on the opposite side. Bring the feet together to locate the middle. Bend the top of the legs to form

a shelf-like structure, running parallel with the base of the feet. This will give the body of the chick something to sit on. Position the body on to the legs and sew to secure.

3 Using the same wrapping method from Step 2, make the beak, but this time when you reach the tip, wrap the yarn back to the middle of the pipe cleaner and bend the tips together. Now wrap more yarn tightly to bind the piece as a whole. Secure the yarn with a stitch and sew on to the head.

4 Glue on two beads for eyes using fabric glue. Give some added character by adding the tips of some yellow marabou feathers to the rear of the chick. Simply dip the tips of the feathers into the glue, push them into the body and leave until dry.

Halloween Pumpkins

Materials:

1 x 100g ball each of bright orange and green yarn

Green felt 4cm (1½in) wide and in the following lengths: 8cm (3¼in), 11cm (4¼in) and 15cm (6in)

Black felt scraps

Green thread

Fabric glue

Tools:

Tailor's chalk

Sizes 45mm (1¾in), 65mm (2½in), and 85mm (3³/₈in) pompom makers

Ruler

Sewing needle

Instructions:

1 To make all of the pumpkin sizes, use a layering technique with the yarns. Select the size of pumpkin you wish to make and open out one side of the maker. Start by adding one layer of green yarn to cover the maker from view. Now cover the green yarn with bright orange until the colour underneath has disappeared. Continue this method of alternating the yarns until the maker is full. Repeat this process for the empty side.

2 Cut and secure the pompom and remove the maker. Trim and shape into a neat ball. With the stripes of your pumpkin running from top to bottom, slightly level the top and bottom to form a more realistic, flatter pumpkin shape.

3 With a ruler, mark and cut out the appropriate size of green felt to complement your pumpkin size. Roll the felt up into a cigar shape along the longest edge and slip stitch into position using green thread. Sew the completed stalk directly into the top of the pumpkin and secure well.

4 Now create the facial expression of your pumpkin using some scraps of black felt. Chalk out spooky mouth and eye shapes, neatly cut them out with fabric scissors, and glue them on.

Christmas Tea Light

Materials:

White yarn

3 x A4 sheets of burgundy felt

Felt scraps in two shades of green

6 large gold sleigh bells

Red satin ribbon 3mm (¹/₈in) x 2m (2¼yd)

One small glass with a 23cm (9in) circumference at the base

Battery-operated tea light (optional)

Tools:

A4 paper

Paper scissors

Tailor's chalk

Size 25mm (1in) pompom maker

Hand sewing needles

Glue gun

Ruler

Compasses

Instructions:

1 Enlarge the mistletoe template (right) to 200 per cent and set aside. Now make your own template for the base of the tea light holder. Set compasses to 7cm (2¾in) wide and draw a circle on to paper. Use the circle to mark out three base sections on to burgundy felt. Neatly cut out all three and layer together, securing with a glue gun. On a separate sheet of A4 felt, mark out a rectangle measuring 12 x 23cm (4¾ x 9in). Cut out and fold together lengthways, gluing to secure, and allow to dry.

2 With some chalk, mark a central line down the folded felt along the longest edge. Using fabric scissors, cut straight lines at 1cm (½in) intervals from the raw edge in towards the chalked line. Bring the short edges together and secure by sewing, but only down to the chalk line. This should form a cuff to grip the base of the glass. The raw edges should fan away from the glass. Placed the cuffed glass centrally onto the base section and glue the

fanned rays to secure into place. Remove the glass so that you can decorate the holder.

3 Make up 6 x 25mm (1in) pompoms in white yarn, trimmed into neat balls. Mark out as many mistletoe leaves in green felt as you require (I have used 6 per shade of green). Cut the ribbon into 30cm (11¾in) lengths and bunch together, securing at the base with a stitch.

4 Now all of your components are ready – pompoms, mistletoe leaves, sleigh bells and ribbon bunches – simply arrange and sew them on to the base. Try a few options first by pinning them down before you decide on a final composition. Please note that if you have a slightly wider bottomed glass, all you have to do is increase the length of the cuff and possibly enlarge the base section a little. Never use a real tea light without the glass.

Note: see page 7 for exact A4 dimensions.

Mistletoe template: Enlarge to 200%

Daisy Decorations

Materials:

Yellow yarn

Pink felt: 2 x A4 sheets per flower

Green garden canes 30cm (11¾in) long

Satin ribbon 3mm (⅛in) in the colour of
your choice

Tools:

A4 paper

Paper scissors

Tailor's chalk

Size 35mm (1⅜in) pompom maker

Glue gun

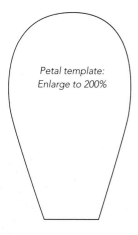

*Petal template:
Enlarge to 200%*

Instructions:

1 First decide how many daisies you wish to make. For each flower you will need to make two 35mm (1⅜in) pompoms. Make up as many pompoms as you require and trim them into neat balls.

2 Enlarge the petal template above by 200 per cent and cut it out. Use it to mark out on the felt as many petals as you require. You will need eight petals per flower. Once marked, cut out and arrange into a fanned circular shape.

3 Secure the petals into position using a glue gun. Add one pompom to the centre front and the other to the back. Attach a length of ribbon to a petal and hang.

4 To make a flower into an alternative plant pot or vase decoration, you will need to cut an extra petal. Before arranging the petals into a circle, glue the cane on to the middle of one of the petals. To conceal the cane, glue a second petal to the top, matching the edges of the petal underneath. You can now arrange the rest of the daisy and add the pompom centres as in Step 3. Gluing the cane in this way will ensure that the flower looks the same on both sides.

Note: see page 7 for exact A4 dimensions.

Lavender Pillows

Materials:

Colourful cotton fabric: two
   pieces of 10 x 15cm (4 x 6in)
   for each pillow

Bright yarn colours to match
   or contrast with fabric

Loose lavender

Sewing thread

Tools:

Tailor's chalk

Size 25mm (1in)
   pompom maker

Sewing machine

Iron

Ruler

Knitting needle

Sewing needle

Instructions:

1 Press fabric flat with a hot iron and, with right sides facing, pin to secure both layers.

2 Set a sewing machine to a medium-sized straight stitch and sew around the piece 1cm (½in) away from the raw edges. Make sure you leave an opening so you are able to turn through and fill with lavender.

3 Before you turn through to the right side, clip the corners and press the seam allowance along the opening side towards the centre. This will give you a nice crisp edge to sew up when you come to close the cushion. Turn through and tease out the corners using a knitting needle. Fill with lavender and slip stitch the opening closed.

4 Now make up four 25mm (1in) pompoms in your chosen yarn. Trim and shape into neat balls. Attach the pompoms to the four corners of the pillow with a needle and thread.

Bobbly Napkin

Materials:

Yarn scraps in your choice
of colours

Cream cotton fabric 41 x
41cm (16¼ x 16¼in)

Sewing threads

Tools:

Tailor's chalk

Size 25mm (1in) pompom maker

Sewing machine

Iron

Ruler

Sewing needle

Instructions:

1 Press the fabric flat with a hot iron. Set your sewing machine to a medium-sized straight stitch to hem the edges of the napkin.

2 You can either use a hemming foot or sew it by hand. Press 5mm (¼in) of fabric over along one edge of the napkin. Repeat this process on the same edge by folding over another 5mm (¼in), hiding the raw edge. Then either machine-sew the fold down, or sew it by hand.

3 Continue until all four sides are completed. Secure any loose threads and cut off the ends.

4 Make up as many pompoms as you require in lots of different bright colours. I have used sixteen in total, spaced around 9cm (3½in) apart. Once the pompoms are made, trim them into neat balls. You will need to make more if you wish the pompoms to sit closer together.

5 Ensure that you space the pompoms evenly. To help with this, attach a pompom to each corner and then to the middle of each side, and so on, until you have an even distribution.

Baby's Room Decorations

Materials:

1 x 100g ball each of baby
   pink and blue yarn

Assortment of matching
   ribbon in different widths

Matching sewing thread

Tools:

Size 45mm (1¾in), 65mm
   (2½in) and 85mm (3³/₈in)
   pompom makers

Ruler

Glue gun

Sewing needles

Instructions:

1 Both of these designs require the same sizes
of pompoms. You can change the colour if
you want to make a neutral one – yellow, for
example. Start by making up one of each of the
three sizes. Trim them into neat balls.

2 The length of each ribbon and the distance
between the pompoms is entirely up to you.
For the pink option, the first pompom has a
40cm (15¾in) drop from the bow and the blue
has a 25cm (9¾in) drop. Each subsequent
pompom is positioned 8cm (3¼in) higher than
the centre of the one below it; the blue version
has two placed at the bottom with the third one
about 8cm (3¼in) higher.

3 Align all of the ribbon tops and secure with
a few stitches. For both versions, add a ribbon
loop to the ribbon tops and stitch into place.
This will allow hanging once finished. Wrap the
sewing thread around the work at this point,
encasing the ribbons. To hide the join tie a
scrap of ribbon towards the front. Tie another
length of ribbon slightly higher than the first
and tie into a bow. Finish by clipping the tails
into an inverted 'v' shape.

4 The blue version is finished in the same way
up to the point of adding the bows. This version
is great for using up offcuts. You will need five
loops: two for the parallel bow, and the other
three to dangle down. Carefully secure the two
parallel loops together using a glue gun and
finish with a scrap over the join. Glue the three
loops neatly to the rear of this ribbon. Cover
the main join with another scrap before adding
the finished bow to the front.

Cup and Ball Toy

Materials:

A4 paper

Yarn scraps in bright colours

Red and white striped cotton

Yellow felt A4 sheets x 2

Red satin ribbon 3mm x 1m
($^1/_8$ x 39½in)

Toy stuffing

Sewing thread

Fabric glue

Tools:

Paper scissors

Tailor's chalk

Size 65mm (2½in)
    pompom maker

Sewing machine

Iron

Sewing needle

Compasses

Ruler

Knitting needle

Pinking shears

Pins

Note: see page 7 for exact A4 dimensions.

Instructions:

1 Start by drawing a template for the cone body. Set compasses to 9cm (3½in) and with an A4 sheet of paper facing you in portrait position, place the pin of the compasses in the bottom left-hand corner. Draw a curve on to the paper. This will form the cone pattern. Cut out and place to one side.

2 Using the cone pattern, cut out two sections in yellow felt and one in a striped cotton. Place the two felt sections together followed by the striped cotton face down. Secure with pins. Set a sewing machine to a medium stitch and sew round the perimeter of the piece 5mm (¼in) away from the raw edge. Make sure you leave an opening to allow turning through. Clip the corners and turn right side out. Tease the corners out with a knitting needle and slip stitch the opening closed. With the cotton striped fabric facing you, topstitch around the entire piece 1cm (½in) from the edge with a sewing machine.

3 Roll the cone up, overlapping the top by 4cm (1½in). Pin to secure. Slip stitch with a needle and thread along the top of the cone and down the body until you reach the tip. Secure. Fill the cone with toy stuffing to about 7–8cm (2¾–3¼in) from the top. Cut a circle measuring 8cm

(3¼in) in diameter from the yellow felt using pinking shears. Glue the circle into the cup to hide the toy stuffing.

4 Make up one 6.5cm (2½in) pompom in bright coloured yarn. After cutting but before removing the pompom maker, tie in the red satin ribbon. Remove the maker and trim the pompom into a neat shape, taking care to avoid the ribbon. Use the slack to attach to the cup with a needle and thread.

Ben the Bear

Materials:

1 x 100g ball each of chocolate brown and caramel yarn

2 x mounted gemstones in black

Black embroidery thread

Scrap of black felt

Tools:

Size 25mm (1in), 35mm (1³/₈in), 45mm (1¾in) and 65mm (2½in) pompom makers

Sewing needle

Glue gun

Instructions:

1 Start by making the bear's ears, head and body. You will need to make two pompoms for the ears with the 25mm (1in) pompom maker, one of 45mm (1¾in) for the head, and one of 65mm (2½in) for the body. Open one half of the pompom maker and wind on the caramel yarn. Fill approximately two-thirds of this side with the caramel colour, and then fill the remaining third with the darker chocolate yarn, completing this half of your maker. Fill the empty side using only the chocolate colour.

2 Repeat this process until you have completed all sizes, then trim and shape the pompoms into neat balls. Attach the head to the body, and then the ears to the head, sewing through the pompoms with yarn for secure anchoring (see photograph for positioning).

3 The paws and feet are made using only the chocolate-coloured yarn. Make two pompoms for the paws with the 35mm (1³/₈in) pompom maker, and two for the feet with the 45mm (1¾in) maker. Trim into neat balls and attach to the body. Position the feet to the front and the paws to the side.

4 Sew on the gemstone eyes and use black embroidery thread for Ben's mouth. Cut a small black felt triangle to create a nose and glue it into position.

Polka Dot Shopper

Materials:

Assorted scraps of brightly coloured yarn

Calico shopping bag, approximately 36cm (14¼in) wide x 42cm (16½in) long

Sewing thread

Tools:

Size 35mm (1³/₈in) pompom maker

Sewing needles or glue gun

Pencil

Ruler

Paper

Instructions:

1 Start by making twenty-five pompoms with a size 35mm (1³/₈in) pompom maker in assorted colours of yarn. Trim and shape all pompoms into neat balls.

2 With a pencil and ruler, mark out a grid on a sheet of paper. The grid should measure 30 x 30cm (11¾ x 11¾in). Divide each side by marking equal intervals of 6cm (2¼in). Join the marks up from left to right and top to bottom. You should now have a grid containing 25 boxes. Mark the centre of each square with a thick pencil dot. These will be used as placement dots for each of the pompoms.

3 Lay the grid pencil-side down on to the centre of the calico shopper and transfer the placement dots by going over them with the pencil from the wrong side. Arrange the pompoms on to the dots. Swap the pompoms around the grid until you are happy with the colour combination. Sew or glue them into position. Using a glue gun will give the pompoms a greater surface area on which to secure them.

Cherry Brooch and Earrings

Materials:

Red and green yarn
Olive embroidery thread
1 x sew-on brooch back
2 x earring hooks

Tools:

Size 25mm (1in) and 35mm
  (1³/₈in) pompom makers
Sewing needle
Knitting dolly (hand-cranked)

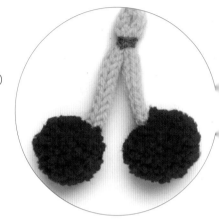

Instructions:

1 Each earring requires two 25mm (1in) pompoms in red yarn. The matching brooch requires two 35mm (1³/₈in)pompoms. Make up the pompoms, then trim them into neat balls.

2 Using a knitting dolly (preferably a hand-cranked one for speed) make up 50cm (19¾in) of braid with the green yarn. Divide this into three sections. For the earrings cut the braid off at 10cm (4in), and 20cm (8in) for the brooch. Once the lengths are cut, finish the raw ends by sewing them closed with matching yarn. Sew a pompom securely on to the ends of the braid.

3 With the pompoms attached, fold the braid in half to locate the middle. Allow one side

to be slightly longer to add character. About 1.5cm (½in) away from the middle point, join the braid together by wrapping embroidery thread around the work to create a band effect.

4 Attach an earring hook to the top of each loop with a needle and thread to finish the earrings.

5 Before attaching the backing to the brooch, slip stitch the braid together about 3cm (1¼in) at the rear to hold the braid closed and hide the metalwork. Then sew the brooch back to the rear of the piece.

Acknowledgements
Alistair would like to thank the team at
Search Press, including May Corfield and
Katie French for their editorial support,
Paul Bricknell for the beautiful photographs,
Marrianne Miall and Juan Hayward for staging
and styling, and everyone supporting me by
buying a copy of my book – I hope you enjoy it!

Publisher's Note
You are invited to visit the author's website:
www.houseofalistair.com